TRANSFORMATION
FROM THE INSIDE OUT

By Alice Sesay Pope

Transformation from The Inside Out

Published by DigitalGenetix Media, 6000 Poplar Avenue, Suite 250, Memphis, TN 38119. Inquiries can be made at www.digitalgenetix.com

ISBN: 9781545577745
First Edition
Printed in the United States of America

Books may be purchased by contacting the publisher and author at:

www.alicesesaypope.com

This book is dedicated to my husband, Edwin Pope who believed in the transformation work that I have contributed to various corporations and influenced me to write this book. I am grateful for the late nights you stayed up with me to write, edit, and research so we could publish this book. You have been the unsung hero to my success.

Thank you.

CONTENTS

ACKNOWLEDGMENT

I would like to thank all the mentors and bosses that gave me the opportunity to lead meaningful initiatives. Furthermore, I am grateful to the teams that I have led through various transformation initiatives—together we achieved big, bold, audacious business results. In addition, I am grateful to my parents, Dr. and Mrs. A. A. Sesay, who provided fantastic examples of a strong work ethic and placed a significant emphasis on education.

More than 40 years ago, my parents made a transformation when they left Sierra Leone, West Africa, came to United States and took steps that changed their legacy forever. They became the first in their immediate family to receive a college degree, become American citizens and instilled the importance of an education to their children. Finally, my parents taught me to dream and believe that through determination and perseverance anything is possible.

To my spiritual mother, Reverend Hattie Saunders Jackson, thank you for praying for me during my high school years, engineering collegiate, graduate studies, and my professional career. To my siblings, Dr. Ola Sesay Abbott and Samuel Sesay, I acknowledge your personal pursuit of excellence and lifelong friendship.

To my children Daryl, Justus, Mitchell, and Xavier: thank you for keeping me on my toes and helping me to calibrate the important things in life. I hope you adopt my customer experience purpose statement that has served me well: "Passion for Excellence—Service from the Heart."

Finally, I want to say thank you to my husband, Edwin Pope. You continually compel me to be transformative not just in a corporate setting, but in all aspects of my life. You made many sacrifices so I could pursue excellence; you motivate me to be the best executive leader. Your guidance and wisdom helped bring this book to fruition. Thank you for your friendship, love, and support.

Your Daughter, Friend, Sister, Mother, and Wife,

Alice

INTRODUCTION

The word *transformation* is often heard, but too many times, it has become little more than a corporate cliché, and lacks substance or impact. This book is designed to provide business leaders and transformational executives with repeatable processes for business transformation that meet or exceed business results. It is for leaders who:

- are brave enough to influence remarkable business change.

- aspire to take their organizations to higher levels.

- realize that a better business model needs to be adopted, different competencies developed, and more aggressive goals established.

- see the big picture and understand the importance of including the customer/member/user experience in their overall corporate strategy.

- are courageous enough to hold themselves and others accountable.

- desire to make the right decisions even when it is

uncomfortable to do so.

Change is not easy to implement. It requires thoughtful planning, the buy-in of the entire organization, and a compelling vision.

Additionally, transformation can sometimes be complex. Some may think of transformation as merely an organizational or technological change. However, true transformational efforts should impact every facet of the company. It requires the participation of the leadership team, each department, vendor, and employee. In short, transformation occurs at both cultural and individual levels.

This book will focus primarily on customer/client/ member experience transformation. Customer experience transformation is a subject area where I possess passion and expertise; therefore, I will provide useful strategies that are relevant and applicable to achieve improved business results.

TRANSFORMATION

"Transformation is a process, and as life happens there are tons of ups and downs. It's a journey of discovery - there are moments on mountaintops and moments in deep valleys of despair." Rick Warren

---

In my early 20s, I was given my first opportunity to lead a manufacturing operations team. When I was offered the position, I was ecstatic. Little did I know how challenging leading people could be! The average tenure of team members in the department was 20 years. The team possessed significant subject matter expertise and had won numerous corporate awards over the years. They were proud of their work and exhibited enormous pride in their results.

Unfortunately, the industry was going through rapid change. Globalization prompted many organizations to find ways to shorten their supply chain cycles and adapt new, more stringent methodologies. The team continued to believe that their efforts were still the best in the industry, and that change wasn't needed. However, production costs had become higher than our competitors. Our competitors were outsourcing manufacturing operations to lower cost facilities in Mexico and Asia to improve their competitive edge.

Morale was low, cost-to-serve was high, and the newly promoted 20-something-year-old (that would be me) had become the new supervisor. The team felt like their world had turned upside down. After all, there was an expectation in the company that one could only become a supervisor after attaining 15 years or more as a top manufacturing operator. At the time, "Don" was the team leader; he had over 26 years of service, strong subject matter expertise and he thought he would be the next supervisor. Don and the team were disappointed that I, a newcomer to the company, had been promoted to the position.

When I started making changes, the team frequently reminisced about the *"way things used to be"*. I was viewed as an outsider. Some members of the team became passive-aggressive and for a while it seemed like we would fail in our efforts to transform the department. However, because I had the buy-in of our executive leadership team and supporting departments, we were able overcome these challenges and build a nimble team that trusted one another.

We lowered costs, improved morale, increased product quality, and quickly reassumed our position as the industry leader. The experience was my first introduction to the complexities of transformation. Does this scenario seem familiar? What I learned for certain is that transformation is not easy.

Transformation is not solely a reorganization, a process improvement initiative, or a cost-cutting exercise. It is a *complete redesign* of a person, product, organization, or concept. It entails taking an organization to a new place and building capabilities that did not previously exist. Technology and businesses change rapidly, thus true transformation should take a person, product, organization, or concept to a new, desired state.

Transformation is all-inclusive

Companies cannot make effective transformations if every facet of the organization doesn't include and reflect the change. In other words, the changes should be easily identified throughout the company by everyone involved. Customers, employees, and even competitors should be able to quickly identify the company shift.

So often companies pay consultants to come in and identify ways to transform the customer/member experience. Many of these recommendations omit seeing things from the customer's point of view, and they do not consider the existing organization culture. A consultant cannot successfully transform the customer experience or any other significant organization change; the people of the company need to be inspired in order to make transformation a success. A transformational effort can save money and improve efficiencies, but that alone does not equate to success. A successful customer experience transformation will increase revenue, decrease customer complaints, reduce risk and improve the overall company profitability.

I can recall a time we introduced an initiative that involved a reorganization of staff, purchasing software, and a planned announcement about the changes we were making. We had lunch catered, a disc jockey, and even commissioned ice sculptures to be used at multiple operation centers. The initiative was considered a resounding success. My leadership team was aglow. A few months later, we realized that we missed a major opportunity to include other organizations in the launch planning and communication event. Therefore, a culture of "we" versus "them" had been created within the same company. It may have been an innocent afterthought but we paid for it for years to come.

Our supporting partners in other departments weren't totally included in the initial strategy. We informed our human resources partners and facilities teams about the changes we wanted to make, but we did not consult them about the way we should approach the change. If we had, our facilities team would have told us to conduct the roll-out when we moved to a new facility. Our human resources team would have also informed us that there were two other business units planning to make similar moves, and we could have created a smoother workflow between departments.

Transformational Failure

Transformational initiatives are not easy, a recent McKinsey & Company research study suggests that 70% of all corporate transformation efforts fail. The research points to three major reasons for transformational failures: -

- Failure to launch: In this stage leaders are unaligned with the vision. There is no clear direction of the problem or the goal. There is employee resistance; both leaders and associates lack accountability. Sometimes failure to launch is due to a lack of funding and the inability to acquire the talent. Transformation needs the right resources to be successful.

- Failure to sustain: Changes are people dependent, not well documented and not automated, so there can be difficulties sustaining transformations over time. The transformation leader might not have been given sufficient leverage, resources or authority to change behaviors. The sustainability of a transformation initiative also fails due to lack of alignment to business metrics and/or budgets.

- Failure to scale: Occurs because the change initiative is not accepted enterprise-wide and lacks senior management backing.

While I have had enormous success in transforming corporate cultures and processes, I have also experienced transformation failures. Most transformational efforts begin with the leaders having great intentions, but missing the mark because of failure to influence the transformation at every company level.

For example, I worked for a company that possessed a great reputation and was generally viewed as being customer-centric. Despite its great reputation, the company faced various industry-specific disruptions. The company frequently lagged behind their competitors in talent, technology, and services. During an executive investment review meeting, I presented a technology implementation that would resolve multiple operational challenges, reduce costs, and dramatically improve customer effort and thus the user experience.

When we presented this implementation, I thought it was a no-brainer because the innovative technology provided benefits with a good return on investment within the first year of implementation. However, one of the more senior executive committee leaders stated that the organization had no desire to lead the industry. He continued that the direction they wanted to take was to be an industry follower and invest in a technology after several other companies had launched it. I was not certain whether this decision was based primarily on budgetary constraints or a flawed corporate strategy. I then wondered if similar conversations had taken place at Blockbuster, Montgomery Ward, Kodak, and Polaroid.

True transformation occurs when people, processes, and technologies are altered. Companies that simply implement the status-quo soon become the status-no! Transformative efforts should occur in response to changing business ecosystems and evolving customer perceptions. If a company simply implements changes that have already been made by its competitors, it will soon face extinction. Every executive leader, department, and employee must be committed to be the best they can be.

Another major contributor to transformational failure

that sometimes leaders fail to appropriately consider is the company politics (sometimes termed as the "culture"). In my experience, egos and politics can kill positive change faster than any budgetary constraint ever could. Transformational leadership must take the political outlook of a company into account. While there is no sure-fire way of addressing this, one should always consider other people's perspectives and situations. I have discovered that no matter how great an idea is, you still must "sell" the idea to overcome individual resistance. Therefore, the abilities to influence, negotiate and compromise become key competencies in reducing transformation resistance.

People should be approached individually in order to acquire diverse insights and explore implementation pros and cons. In some instances, I provide incentives for the change to gain support. Corporate politics is an abstract science, but it must be taken into consideration if an initiative is going to be approved and sustainable over time.

<u>Your Turn</u>:

- Can you identify an opportunity for improvement that would shift the corporate culture?

- Have you ever experienced transformation failure, what did you learn from the experience?

<u>Reflection:</u>

What is the most memorable business transformation that you have experienced? Why was it memorable?

MASS-LEVEL EXTINCTION EVENTS

"Customers decide whether your product or service becomes relevant or extinct". -- Alice Sesay Pope

---

Consumers have information at their fingertips and will often conduct research about a company before they purchase a product or service. Websites like Google's My Business and Yelp! enable customers to review the experiences of other customers and decide whether to purchase a product or to take their business elsewhere. Even a company's reputation as an employer is subject to intense scrutiny. Potential employees can review employer ranking websites like Glassdoor to see what a company's employees think about that company. With the research and review tools available to consumers, transformation becomes more than a buzzword, it becomes a necessary process to keep up with changing customer expectations. The importance of creating a corporate culture that first "listens" to the voice of the customer and is "agile" enough to make the necessary changes cannot be underestimated.

When customers' needs and expectations are unfulfilled, the likelihood that they will choose an alternative product or service is high. The warp speed pace of transformation makes every industry vulnerable to fatal disruptions. There's an extensive list of companies throughout history that didn't recognize that they were about to experience an MLEE: A Mass Level Extinction Event. This simply means a disruptive innovation was created and companies that did not respond fast enough became victimized by corporate Darwinism.

Eastman Kodak, a company I am personally fond of, is one of the more notable companies listed in Figure 1. How does a company like Kodak, once consistently listed as a Fortune 30 company with over 100 years of dominance, and one of the largest portfolios of patents in the world lose its prominence in today's business world? It is quite simple: It failed to recognize changing industry ecosystems and customer expectations.

The table below gives a few notable examples of technology disruption MLEEs.

Once a Pioneer	Shut down by Digital Transformation
Kodak film	Digital cameras and cell phones
Phone Landlines and pay phones	Cell Phones
BlockBuster	Netflix
Travel Agencies	Online Travel
Retail Stores	Amazon
Taxi cabs	Uber and Lyft
Traditional Hotels	Airbnb

Figure 1: Technology Disruptors

Modern technology poses a threat to all companies. Kodak is notable because of the high profit margins associated with manufacturing a roll of film. Kodak's senior leadership understood that rolls of film, paper and film chemicals were a major source of corporate revenue. They did not want to release digital cameras to the market because it would cannibalize the revenues made from film products. Kodak held the patents for digital photography, but didn't move at a fast-enough pace to meet changing customer expectations. As a matter of fact, Kodak developed the first digital camera in 1975, over twenty years before digital cameras become an imminent MLEE. What was the dilemma? Kodak did not properly quantify the economic outcomes of changing customer expectations against the potential of lost revenue.

Kodak's demise as an industry leader illustrates the danger in ignoring the financial risk of not changing. Kodak executives attempted to identify customer expectations only after significant market share losses to forward-thinking companies like Sony. It is unfortunate that Kodak did not have access to the current real-time metrics we have today to analyze the "voice of the customer" against short and long-term economic value. Many leaders feel it is not in their best interest to invest in transformational efforts because they have not connected the effect of change with the bottom line. However, it is important to evaluate the economic and qualitative impact before a solid business decision can be made. Simply denying an initiative that could provide a stronger customer experience and drive demand is counter-productive.

Avoiding MLEEs

Competitive companies evolve at every level. A transformational organization fosters innovation, makes investments, and creates an environment where outside-of-the-box thinking is encouraged. Processes become digitized, standardized, and well documented with a clear end-to-end enterprise journey. This eliminates possible dysfunctions that can occur with broken processes.

Changes are sometimes required because of shifts in customer preferences. Technology is an evolving paradigm and requires organizations to adapt quickly. Companies that add value by accelerating change, and simplifying the customer experience position themselves to gain greater market share.

No industry today is exempt from experiencing a possible MLEE. For that reason, bank leaders are making changes to business models to keep up with technology and customer expectations. There was a time when customers had long term relationships with their bankers and could simply drive to a bank branch to talk with a person they trusted. The idea of frequent visits to a branch is becoming a distant memory, yet bankers still need to create a trusted relationship with their customers. A recent study commissioned by Google entitled "How people use their phones for finance activities" shows that 4 in 10 smartphone owners turn to their phones to conduct financial activities instead of going to a bank branch. In recent years, the brick and mortar model is inadequate in capturing full customer engagement. This shift in customer behavior has propelled the creation of mobile applications that help consumers to manage stock portfolios, apply for loans, and to purchase items in retail outlets instead of using credit cards.

The speed and strategies that financial institutions employ will dictate the amount of market share they keep and the amount lost to fintech companies. No industry is exempt from transformative disruptions; MLEEs are indiscriminate. Banks, too are finding ways to transform their core operating models by empowering employees, listening to their customers, and improving accessibility and transparency.

Your Turn:

- Have you ever experienced working in a company on the verge of becoming an MLEE?

- What is your takeaway regarding MLEEs?

Reflection:

Was there ever a time that you felt your organization was facing an MLEE? Why, or why not?

PEOPLE

In the next chapters, we will cover the three pillars of transformation. People, Processes, and Technology. All three pillars can help usher in positive change. It is my experience that the most important of the three Transformation Pillars is the People Pillar.

People in a company make the difference to a successful

transformation. Companies can share the same processes and technologies but not realize the same results without associate engagement. During the 1990's dotcom boom, the spread of the Internet and the Telecommunications Act of 1996 brought retailers into the homes of millions of consumers. Internet retailers and telecom companies sprang up overnight. Companies like Pets.com, Lycos, eToys.com, Books-a-Million, and Amazon were born and thrived during this era. However, by the end of 2001 many of these companies became victims of an MLEE.

AMAZON

What was the difference between thriving and extinction? Leadership. Amazon is a notable example of a company that has consistently transformed its business model to provide a simpler, faster, cheaper model for customers. They now dominate the retail industry.

There are countless books and case studies that document Amazon's rise to prominence. Since 1994, Amazon's ability to diversify and dominate the retail industry is unprecedented. How did a dotcom company that started out selling books become such a dominant power? In my research of various dotcom companies, Amazon stands out.

Many Amazon naysayers tout the fact that Amazon was

created on a platform of change in the nineties: the Internet. However, that idea is negated by the failure of similar web-based companies such as Books-A-Million and Kozmo.com that started during the same timeframe. Amazon's meteoric rise points to one consistency: visionary leadership. Jeff Bezos, founder and CEO of Amazon, knew what he wanted to accomplish, so invested in a long-term strategy. In Bezos' very first letter to shareholders in 1997, he declared "We will continue to focus relentlessly on our customers". A customer-centric culture from the start, Amazon built transformation into its cultural DNA and placed customers at the focus of all business strategies.

Therefore, Amazon products are now household words. Amazon Kindle ®, Amazon Instant Video ®, Amazon Fire ®, Alexa ®, Zappos, and of course, the game-changing Amazon Prime ®. Bezos implemented constant evaluations of every facet of his company. From innovative inventory technologies, to becoming the leader of customer expectations, Bezos has built a disciplined customer-centric organization focused on continuous improvement. It's no surprise that in 2015, Amazon became the fastest company to reach $100 billion in annual sales. Amazon leaders did not accept the idea of becoming a victim of an MLEE, rather they served as an instigator of MLEEs.

TRANSFORMATIONAL LEADERSHIP

"Effort and change are not enough without purpose and direction" -- John F. Kennedy

---

Transformation can be fostered in an organization with the introduction of a new internal or external leader. Often, a change in leadership is one of the fastest methods of fostering transformation. Let us examine a professional sports team to illustrate the impact a new leader brings to a franchise that aspires to attain a greater accomplishment. I am an avid sports fan, so I'll reference a basketball team I admire in order to provide an example of the transformative impact of leadership.

Gregg "Pop" Popovich originally joined the San Antonio Spurs as an assistant coach under Larry Brown in 1988. Popovich, was later let go from the Spurs in 1992 but he was hired to work under another legendary head coach, Don Nelson of the Golden State Warriors.

The San Antonio Spurs was a decent team; they drafted

David "The Admiral" Robinson in 1987 (even though they had to wait for two years until he completed his military obligation with the Navy), and they finished fourth in the Western Conference the year before. Popovich was brought back to the San Antonio franchise as the general manager in 1994 and rapidly transformed the culture.

Popovich injected a culture of teamwork by establishing clear team goals, implementing a strong player skills development program, and recruiting diverse talent from various countries to fit the Spurs strategic plan. Popovich later understood that he could not completely fulfill his dual role as coach and general manager, and promoted R. C. Buford, a long time Spurs scout, to the general manager role.

Gregg Popovich still coaches the San Antonio Spurs and they continue to be relevant, despite the retirement of David Robinson and perennial All-Star Power Forward Tim Duncan. Popovich serves as an example of the impact that the right person in the right role at the right time can have on moving an organization from mediocre to great!

I enjoy watching professional sports and observing the teams that transform from good to great when a new leader comes along, unfortunately sometimes teams with a new leader transition from bad to worse. Consider Seattle Seahawks coach

Pete Carroll. He tried to transform the NY Jets in 1994 and failed. He was fired, and later became head coach of the New England Patriots from 1997-1999; that did not go too well either. He finally became a winning coach for several years at the University of Southern California (USC) and won the 2014 Super bowl as head coach of the Seattle Seahawks.

In professional sports, some teams change coaches frequently but never gain the desired results. Although the leader is critical to transformation, the new coach is not the only factor. There are many crucial factors required to create a winning team or successful business. These factors are:

- Recruit: Recruit, develop and retain a team that believes in the change.

- Inspire: Share a compelling reason for transformation, in other words capture the hearts of the team, inspire them.

- Lead: Lead teams through the change curve

- Realign: Realign talent or fire transformation detractors.

Recruit: when transformation is desired, the competencies for the job usually change as well. Sometimes the right competencies are more important than subject matter expertise. It is up to the leader to redesign the requirements of the role and to define a new job description. For instance, when I began managing large contact center organizations, my recruiters would send resumes of applicants with prior contact center or specific industry experience. However, we later discovered that the best contact center professionals were the ones that were extremely friendly, flexible, critical thinkers and passionate about customer experience. After the recruiting process is completed, the transformation is successful when a culture is created that retains the associates.

Inspire: If leaders can capture the hearts of the people, the people will follow the transformation initiative with passion and tenacity. The inspiration needs to be sincere and genuine, with a win-win for all parties involved.

Lead: Even though the right people, inspired by the transformation, are in place, change is hard. Good leaders spend time listening, communicating, and reiterating the importance of the transformation process.

Realign: One of the toughest processes for me is reorganizing an organization. Sometimes it means that some people are redeployed or—even worse—lose their jobs. However, there are times when a few people refuse to join the transformation journey; they whine about "who moved their cheese". Don't give up on detractors immediately, but if you are spending more time with detractors versus the rest of the people in the organization—that might be a sign that it's time to do something different. I am not heartless by any means, I spend sleepless nights pondering a decision that might impact the livelihood of others before acting. However, detractors tend to create negative energy that is destructive to the entire team.

Toxic Leadership Can Inspire Negative Change

In one of my former roles, an external executive (for anonymity let's call her Irene) was hired to lead various operations. I was excited, the leader had received an Ivy League education and worked with top companies in our industry. At the time, our company had grown due to multiple acquisitions, and my team had received various internal and external customer service and sales awards. Thus, there was a positive buzz throughout the entire company. The opportunity to learn from another leader was enticing. Unfortunately, my excitement was short lived.

In less than a month after Irene was hired, people were

running for the hills. Without conducting detailed assessments or communicating with members of her leadership team, she started firing people. In less than six months, Irene fired top leaders, lost the confidence of the people and put the company through four major organization changes. Because our department functions were tied to government regulatory compliance, replacing these leaders was tough. The first year, Irene was over budget by approximately $10 million dollars! In addition, after key leaders left, the company faced regulatory violations. It is interesting that Irene had spent most of her career at a company plagued with one of the largest regulatory violation payouts.

The team was disappointed that Irene failed to assess the operations and develop a strategic transformation road map with a collaborative cross functional team. Furthermore, she didn't communicate effectively with her cross-functional peers. The team felt like being in an episode of Game of Thrones. You never knew when your time was up.

Transformation for the sake of transforming can be toxic. A transformational leader provides unobstructed vision, communicates effectively with everyone involved, and is empathic to the customer perspective. The most painful part of Irene's transformation initiative is that she hired and promoted unqualified people. The organization became chaotic and people were back biting, lying and doing whatever they could so they would not be the next person fired. The business environment became toxic. People started focusing on the drama going on at work instead of working to satisfy the customer.

I remember she conducted several layoffs and provided individuals with lucrative severance packages. The funny thing is that everyone she laid off acquired new external roles within weeks, took the package, and the company lost significant subject matter expertise. After making a big mess, she left the company and returned to the west coast.

Why did this leader fail? Irene's changes were personal and political instead of enterprise-wide and strategic. Her efforts were about her making her mark. The point of the story is to avoid self-centered and overzealous ambitions; instead, manage with a clear strategic road map, and in the company's best interest.

Successful transformation is a deliberate, strategic action that creates an ecosystem which factors in people, processes, and technology to significantly improve business outcomes. Since it is a dramatic shift, it is difficult and sometimes painful to execute. The toughest factor to manage in transformation is the people—at all levels—peers, employees, and senior leaders. It is like a chess game ,and moves must be made with great thought, consideration, and caution, with the understanding that transformation is necessary in order to remain competitive.

As organizations transform, we too must change. Leaders must undergo personal change as well as equipping their teams to embrace transformation and follow the change model. Being a leader of transformation has forced me to undergo personal transformation. Effective leadership embraces change, even when change conflicts with personal desires and makes us uncomfortable.

Where Does Transformational Leadership Begin?

Transformation begins with you. It is the realization that a dramatic shift needs to occur and more than the status quo is desired. Once the desired status has been defined, the next steps involve getting the right stakeholders involved and creating a high-level overview of what it will take to arrive at the desired state. The leader conveys the transformational initiative to the entire company. This can take the form of an internal positioning theme or motto that succinctly reflects the core intent of the initiative. If the organization doesn't have a positioning theme, become the leader that establishes it.

The following positioning themes are examples that have informed and empowered corporate cultures to achieve their objectives:

Amazon: Our vision is to be the most customer-centric company; to build a place where people can come to find and discover anything they want to buy online.

Capital One: Change banking for good.

Nike: To bring inspiration and innovation to every athlete in the world.

Apple: We believe technology should lift humanity and enrich people's lives in all the ways people want to experience it.

Starbucks: To inspire and nurture the human spirit— one person, one cup and one neighborhood at a time.

As you read, each positioning theme/mission statement, it is quite clear that the companies mentioned above have lived up to their mission statements. It takes time to build a compelling mission statement and acquire widespread buy-in. The words of an effective mission statement should be words that people live by and utilize in making business decisions.

Your Turn:

- What actions are your company taking that are counterproductive to the mission statement?

- What keeps you from being a transformational leader?

- What are the current challenges to fulfilling the positioning theme/mission statement?

Reflection:

Have you ever worked for a transformational leader? What was transformational about him or her?

CULTURE SHIFT

"You have to maintain a culture of transformation and stay true to your values." - Jeff Weiner

Changing a standing corporate culture is difficult. In most instances, the people that have brought you in recognize the need for change, but they can also be the reason the change is needed. It's been my experience that the executives that were keen to promote you or hire you may not fully understand their own personal biases to the cultural obstacles. Proceed with caution!

I remember being brought in to develop a plan to improve the social media presence of a corporation. I was excited because there was a litany of opportunities and I felt the plan would be a slam dunk. I presented the plan, and although it was accepted, I later received criticism that I made a leader that had been responsible for the social media strategy "look bad".

Wow, I was amazed, I had discussed the opportunities and included members of each team. I thought I had dotted each 'i' and crossed every 't', however I did not take the corporation's existing culture into consideration. It was obvious that the company had created a family atmosphere, but I did not realize the power of the existing culture. As a result, my surefire plan took longer to implement and I was temporarily placed on the "bad" executive list. If you have ever experienced a similar situation, don't get discouraged, transformational leaders are frequently misunderstood.

Before driving transformation, learn and understand the corporate culture; this is the cumulative sum of attitudes, customs, and beliefs unique to a group of people. A clear understanding of the culture will determine the transformation's effectiveness.

In some instances, there are cultural norms that must be re-evaluated and challenged. However, there are intricate factors of culture that are fundamental to the company's core values, making it critical to the organization's fabric.

A transformational leader evaluates the cultural components that need to be changed, and the cultural norms that need to be maintained. A great rule of thumb is to spend extensive time building relationships before making major changes, so intent is not skewed. Transformation is both a science and an art. The science part is clearly understanding the problem(s) and solving it. The art requires understanding people and culture.

Great transformational leaders do not have to be subject matter experts. However, they need to be able to connect with others and ask the right questions. Leading people means understanding behaviors, goals, and motivations. Most of all, true transformational leadership requires gaining insight into what inspires individuals and teams to stretch beyond the status quo. This does not mean becoming the best friend of everyone on the team. Frankly speaking, transformational leaders may not have a ton of friends, because they make others dwelling in the status quo uncomfortable. However, when you lead with integrity and make sound business decisions, you will eventually gain the respect of various people throughout the organization.

Furthermore, successful transformational leaders acquire the buy-in of people in the organization by inspiring them to embrace the journey. Total buy-in does not happen overnight because it requires trust to be built. The best of plans cannot be successfully created and executed if the entire company doesn't view the transformation as a win-win scenario. Leaders must develop plans to overcome resistance to change. Deliberate communication and enterprise-wide involvement in the transformation strategy lowers tension levels. Each person has a critical role to the organization's success, in influencing others in order to understand their individual contributions to the business goals and objectives.

Trust is critical because anxieties can run high when change occurs. People are fearful that transformation initiatives could eliminate their roles or make them look bad. Others might resist transformation because they don't feel they were involved in the process, and don't have confidence in an outsider.

Strong leadership can help others acclimate to a corporate culture shift. If people see the change in you, and also see your confidence in the transformation, they are more likely to buy in to the change as well. For example, before you roll out new accountability metrics for your team, create and broadcast metrics for yourself. This helps to gain allies and influencers. Building relationships can be done during roundtables, lunch, or simply over a cup of coffee. Let people know you care about them, learn about their career paths and the organization history.

During this time of building relationships, listen carefully. The process of building relationships never ends; it should be done continually. I recommend building trust with peers, direct reports and department heads. In the process, share information about yourself as well. Building trust will not happen overnight, but lead by example. Let your actions demonstrate authenticity and sincerity. One way to do this is by creating enterprise solutions and breaking silo barriers.

Once the right partnerships are developed, and people have embraced the transformation goals, cultural challenges need to be addressed. The company culture needs to support the transformation vision. In addition, the environment must support a culture that provides associates with the right training, tools, incentives, and competencies to facilitate transformation. For instance, at one company there was pride in the accomplishments over the years, and although those accomplishments were no longer relevant to the current business scenario, it was important to acknowledge past contributions.

<u>Your Turn</u>:

- What are the most important cultural characteristics of your organization?

- What cultural norms are important to keep?

- Every organization has great cultural components that are valuable. What cultural norm does your team need to break? Why?

<u>Reflection</u>:

Has a cultural norm ever paralyzed a transformation event? Why, or why not?

TECHNOLOGY

TECHNOLOGY

"With digital transformation, the consumer, rather than the technology, is in the driver's seat, and this matters." -Forbes

We are in a world driven by technology. Leaders that desire to manage sweeping transformation should create a digital strategy as a part of their transformation plan. Technology innovation makes it possible to generate differentiated or new customer value.

The impact of technology is tremendous. We use it to do pretty much everything. I use my smartphone as an alarm clock, but I also call on "Alexa" (the Amazon artificial intelligence assistant) to acquire weather information for the day and top news. I send and receive money through electronic payment systems like Zelle and Square Cash. We can even remotely answer our front door even when we are in another country through our doorbell app. Technology has leveled the playing field for companies of all sizes all over the world.

As a result of these technological advancements, customer expectations are high. As a customer experience leader, it is a challenge to deliver an outstanding customer experience that continues to entice customers into staying while working within regulatory and financial constraints.

Digital solutions have transformed the education system, as well as healthcare, agriculture, finance, real estate, retail, travel, and the list goes on. Digital solutions are expected by consumers, so leaders should evaluate current solutions and ensure that they are implemented effectively.

The digital revolution has led to unprecedented innovation. Companies are implementing new technologies to keep up, but a new technology alone does not lead to digital transformation unless it enhances the user experience and creates a competitive advantage.

Digital solutions are key to transforming the customer experience. Forrester defines digital businesses as "those that win, serve, and retain customers by continuously creating and exploiting digital assets to simultaneously deliver new sources of customer value and increase their operational agility."

Digital transformation requires the ability to change business models by digitizing the customer experience in ways that deliver a differentiated experience, increase customer engagement, provide new upsell opportunities, and establish loyalty to the customer through a deep emotional connection that makes it difficult for insurgents to gain market share.

Through digital transformation, leaders create a digital technology across the value stream. This requires digitizing the end-to-end customer journey and building an API (application program interface) strategy.

APIs connect various software programs to provide a seamless experience. Since technology evolves rapidly and the cost of implementation is high, successful transformational leaders develop a strategy that connects the customer experience at the enterprise level. Technology investments are high, so transformation leaders must carefully evaluate the feasibility of the short term and long-term implications of each technology purchase. The API strategy should seamlessly enable connectivity across the customer journey.

The impact of digital technology has permanently altered the way we approach customer experience. Digital innovations have heightened customer awareness and expectations. As we think about the digital transformation impact on businesses, it is important to factor in the rapid rise of mobile usage.

With the proliferation of innumerable social media

channels and improved mobile devices, customers are hyper-connected. According to a 2017 report by ComScore, 71% of the American population owns a mobile phone. In 2014, mobile usage surpassed desktop usage in the United States. Consumers are using mobile phones to search, click, swipe, play, and even pay. Have you noticed that most mobile phone owners typically have their phone within their reach? Why is this important? Transformation leaders must have a mobile strategy to reach a larger customer base.

Corporate leaders face the dilemma of selecting the right platform and addressing changing customer expectations, while meeting profitability guidelines. The fast adoption of mobile usage and the mobile "phone addiction" of our culture has drastically increased customer requirements. As digital features are continually being enhanced across geographies and industries, more customer service and sales transactions occur digitally.

Because of disruptive technologies, companies no longer define the value of their brand—customers do. Consumers want an experience that is customized to their needs and wants, both explicit and implied. Simply put, people want companies they do business with to touch them on their channel of choice and to meet their evolving needs. How can a company keep up with these continuous changes?

As a customer experience executive, I am constantly challenged with keeping pace with customer expectations, operating within budgetary guidelines, and selecting the right technology for the industry, geography, and customer base.

Digital transformation is more than selecting a technology to implement. A large Fortune 50 software company recently rolled out digital transformation promotions to its customers and outlined digital transformation in terms of four categories:

- Engaging customers/citizens

- Empowering employees

- Optimizing operations

- Transforming products and services

The fast pace of digital transformation is challenging to manage for numerous reasons. For a start, there are many software vendors and consultants offering solutions. Since digital transformation is a major focus of most companies, businesses want to gain market share with an offering.

Most of these offerings come with hefty price tags—in the millions of dollars. For instance, in an omni-channel contact center, investments need to be made to add further automation through chat bots, machine learning, biometrics technology etc. For example, biometrics technology transforms the customer experience by enabling fingerprint and even voice authentication. There are automated solutions that capture enterprise customer journeys in real time.

It doesn't stop there. We now have data—and lots of it. Customer experience transformation leaders must decide on the data that is actionable, and enables greater insight in attaining desired business outcomes.

- How does your company determine when it is necessary to make a technology investment?

- Does your company possess a technology competitive edge?

Reflection:

Has your company implemented a technology innovation that became a disruptor? What was unique about it, and how did it increase the customer base and revenues?

PROCESSES

APPLYING SIX-SIGMA

"If you can't describe what you are doing as a process, you don't know what you're doing." -W. Edwards Deming

---

Have you ever attended a meeting that provided a forum for great discussions about a strategy to transform an organization? After the meeting, you felt energized that change was on its way. However, no one took notes, outlined roles and responsibilities, or drew up a map to attain transformation results. There might have even been subsequent meetings and some improvements made, but the results fell short of the full opportunity.

It is important to create a strategic road map when leading sweeping transformation. I recommend a six-sigma approach. Scrum and sprints are useful for software updates and can be included within the overall road map. A scrum/sprint methodology does not replace a six-sigma plan, or the overarching road map. Since people may not be familiar with utilizing a six-sigma approach for transformation plans, I have outlined the steps.

I have been fortunate to learn and benefit from a robust six-sigma methodology approach. I have received training from General Electric (GE) master black belts and practiced at process-driven organizations. We will explore a high-level overview of six-sigma utilized during a transformation initiative.

I recommend six-sigma methodology for transformation because I know it works. Although it is still beneficial to utilize sprints or scrum philosophy for software development, a transformation initiative needs to be clearly mapped out to factor in various objectives and to provide a path to operational excellence.

The six-sigma methodology does not have to be utilized for a transformation initiative, but it provides a great framework in which to keep track of complex process action items. Make an honest examination (the good, bad, and ugly) of the challenges and/or the goals that need to be accomplished.

Let's start by translating a transformation initiative to a six-sigma process. Another reason why six-sigma methodology is advantageous, is because practitioners focus on metrics and repeatable processes that are sustainable over time. If executed properly, it provides a good return on investment.

The six-sigma Define, Measure, Analyze, Improve and Control (DMAIC) process aims at improving *existing* business processes. The Define, Measure, Analyze, Design and Verify (DMADV) process is used for creating *new* products or processes. The first three phases of DMADV and DMAIC are the same.

The DMAIC process is composed of five phases:

Figure 2: Six-sigma Process Flow

The six-sigma process improvement strategy occurs within a team environment. Therefore six-sigma initiatives require the participation of a cross-functional team to gain understanding of the problem, and ultimately to lead to the best possible scenarios. The table below represents a high-level overview of the six sigma tools that we'll explore in more detail:

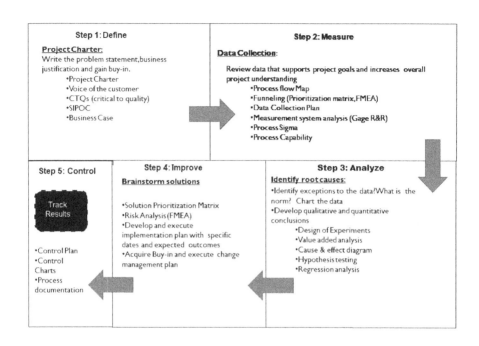

Figure 3: Six-sigma Process Steps

Lean and six-sigma are sometimes used in the same context; both are process improvement methodoliges but have separate meanings. Six-sigma is a set of management techniques intended to improve business processes by greatly reducing the probability that an error or defect will occur. The term "lean" means to eliminate sources of waste or "Muda" in Japanese. The term "lean" comes from the Japanese term 改善 "kaizen", which means improvement or take apart to make new. The focus of kaizen initiatives is to eliminate waste, which is categorized in seven forms, (a straightforward way to remember is the phrase TIMWOOD):

1. Transportation

2. Inventory

3. Motion

4. Waiting

5. Overproduction

6. Over processing

7. Defects

Transportation – An inefficient way of moving items or people. For example, taking documents to another employee for signature versus sending an e-signature.

Inventory – Purchasing or making things before they are needed, things waiting in an (electronic or physical) inbox. Piles of anything before it is needed. In a service organization, it can mean staffing associates when the volume is not needed.

Motion – Any excess movement by human workers, for example walking to a copier, printer, fax, central filing, shuffling through papers or searching for missing information. This also includes shifting back and forth between computer screens.

Waiting (or Time delay) – Can either be time when no action is taken, or when the process is stopped, which can be due to waiting for decision makers, subject matter experts, technology down time etc. This is additional time added to the process for an upstream process to deliver, for a machine to finish processing, for a supporting function to be completed, or for an interrupted worker to get back to work.

Over-production – Taking action that is unnecessary or not needed to meet the customer's needs. For example, creating several folders which hold the same files, making irrelevant reports.

Over-processing – Ineffective procedures which result in poor outcomes. For example, depending on inspections or quality audits rather than designing a process to eliminate problems. This usually happens because root cause problems have not been eliminated.

Defects – Errors made that cause the customer to be dissatisfied. Because of a defect the product or service does not provide the intended result. For instance, a customer deposits cash into an ATM but the customer's account balance does not show the balance.

DEFINE

"If I were given one hour to save the planet, I would spend 59 minutes defining the problem and one minute resolving it."

Albert Einstein

The define phase enables development of a well-defined charter and problem statement that can be communicated and shared throughout the organization. At the start of a project, the charter is created to outline what needs to be accomplished, and to decide how the project is going to proceed. A problem statement is the articulation of the issues that need to be resolved. After stating the issue, explain why it's a big deal— after all, no one has the time or resources to try to solve every single minor problem. Outline the business rationale for the six-sigma methodology and how it improves the transformation initiative.

A well-defined team charter and problem statement eliminates any confusion about the initiative and enables the team to focus on the business outcomes. After capturing the problem statement, pull together a project charter that includes:

- Problem statement

- Project scope

- Business goals (with quantitative metrics)

- Timelines for each phase

- Project resources: team and executive

It is possible to modify or change the project charter based on developments during the initiative. However, the project business case should be compelling, and linked to business goals and objectives. Likewise, the goal statement should meet the SMART criteria (specific, measurable, attainable, relevant, and time-bound). Furthermore, clearly outline roles and responsibilities; then document it.

To strengthen the problem statement, define a clear project scope that:

- Defines boundaries of the scope

- Establishes a start and end

- Ensures the project scope is manageable

- Removes constraints that might impact the team

- Consists of quantitative metrics as well as qualitative descriptions

The estimated project completion date should have a structured plan, Gantt chart, or similar project management tool. Finally, the communication plan must determine when to share critical content, distribution lists, and methods of communication (SharePoint sites, emails, newsletters, intranet sites, etc.).

Voice-of-the-Customer (VOC)

The internal or external customer is the focus of the improvement opportunity. Therefore, start by understanding the customer's needs; review customer complaints, walk in the shoes of the customer, and most of all, use the company's products and services. VOC can be found through employee interviews, workshops, surveys, customer interviews, observation, journals, social media comments, website analytics, third party review sites, call center recordings, call center agent notes, and inbound emails. The focus is ultimately the external customer, however, some roles do not necessarily interact with an external customer, but an impact on an internal customer can have a downstream impact on an external customer.

Find out customer pain points from associates who interact with customers on a regular basis. These associates will know the cumbersome internal business practices that make it difficult to deliver a great customer experience. Find out what is important to the customer, and what is critical to quality (CTQs). Most of all, gain a deep understanding of customer complaints.

It is sometimes easy to identify hypothetical issues, but discovering the organization's true problems requires a systematic approach. To do so effectively, roll up your sleeves; spend time in various organizations, especially ones outside your direct span of control.

Talk to the people at all levels to acquire a balanced view of the organization. Visit multiple operations that impact the customer experience: contact center agents, retail representatives, back office operations, fulfillment agents, and all representatives that interact directly with customers.

Collect quantitative and qualitative data points relating to the problem. Ask lots of clarifying questions to get to the root cause and not merely surface issues; listen well, and take detailed notes. When sufficient information has been collected, write down the problem statement using qualitative and quantitative information.

Here are two examples of problem statements: -

1. The software development team has been unable to meet delivery launch dates for the past 18 months. Major initiatives have been late by 3-6 months. The delay of product launches causes the project to go over budget by 20% (or over $1 million). Furthermore, there is a high attrition rate of 18.2% on the development team, and morale is low. Finally, product launch delays have an estimated revenue loss of potentially 20 million dollars annually.

2. The contact center handles 90% of transactions via the phone channel, which is a prohibitive cost to serve. Furthermore, customers' issues are not resolved during the first call and there are repeat callers. The service level for the phone channel is not consistently met because there is a high attrition rate of 53%. There are competing contact centers within 10 miles of the center that pay a higher wage and provide better benefits. The contact center is not meeting service levels and there is a 10-point drop in net promoter score (NPS).

After capturing the problem statement, develop a SIPOC (Suppliers, Input, Process, Output, Customers) of the end-to-end process you are improving. The SIPOC outlines dependencies to the problem statement by addressing questions such as:

- Who is the suppler?

- Are there vendors?

- What are the inputs to the process?

- Are there other departments in the organization that contribute to the process?

- What is the output of the process?

- What business output do you desire?

- What business output are you getting now?

Finally, it is important to know your customers and know what delights them.

SIPOC

Draw the current state of a process (not what you aspire to, but what the process looks like today). One way to do this is by using a SIPOC diagram. Start by mapping the process.

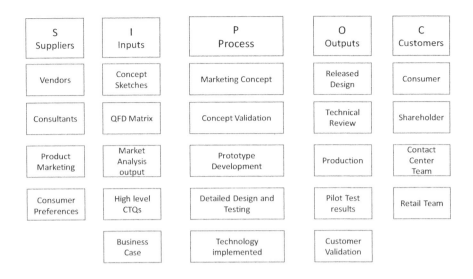

Figure 4: SIPOC Diagram

Identify Quick Wins

Before rushing to the next phase, identify quick wins. After outlining the project charter, there might be a few process improvements that the team should implement quickly. Don't skip the value of following the six-sigma process, but at the same time, don't delay an obvious process improvement opportunity—especially if it is easy to execute.

Although some problems will require additional resources and technology to improve, some changes are simple; I call those "quick- wins- now" opportunities. It could be as simple as increasing the empowerment of a group of associates to eliminate waiting, rework, and other non-value-added activities.

"Quick- wins- now" opportunities typically are easy to implement and lead to immediate efficiency gains, associate satisfaction, and customer improvement opportunities.

Here is an example of a "quick- wins- now" opportunity: A contact center team tries to improve the time taken to resolve customer issues, so they focus on improving average handle time (AHT). One of the managers realizes that the handle time is high when associates navigate through various computer screens which slow down the process.   Someone on the team has an idea to provide agents with dual monitors in order to reduce AHT. The team conducts a pilot with a small team of agents, and in a one-week period, all agents achieved a 25% reduction in AHT. The cost of the additional monitors is approximately $20,000.00 for the team of 100 agents, but it would reduce annual headcount by 10 people or provide additional capacity for training purposes. The return on investment is immediate. The dual monitors paid for themselves within the first four months. Do you wait to go through the DMAIC process to implement? Absolutely not! It's a no brainier.

<u>Your Turn</u>:

- What methods do your organization use to ensure projects are implemented in a robust manner?

- What major problem is your organization facing? Write the problem statement.

What's holding you from leading the implementation of an obvious improvement opportunity?

<u>Reflection:</u>

Was there a time that a great idea or transformation was poorly executed? What went wrong?

MEASURE

The measure phase is designed to acquire quantifiable evaluation of characteristics/level of performance based on observable data. During the measure phase, create a data collection plan. Find the data that tells the story and conveys the end-to-end customer journey. Determine the data points that provide a greater understanding of the problem statement, hypothesis, current state and future state. In addition, the data collection plan provides metrics that enable the team to gauge the improvement opportunity.

A sample data collection data plan is listed in the table below:

Sample Data Collection Plan					
Performance Measure	Operational Definition	How will the data be collected	Who will collect the data	When will the data be collected	Sample size
VOC					
Financials					
Process					
Others					
Others					

Figure 5: Collection Plan

Map the process with cross-functional team members. You may know departmental processes, but transforming an organization's customer experience requires interdependence at the enterprise level. One of the most productive ways to begin the mapping process is to hold a project kick-off. Identify key stakeholders and subject matter experts and invite them to a four- to eight-hour session where everyone can collectively make contributions.

In addition, this phase is used to calculate the process capability. Furthermore, it is a good practice to benchmark other processes internally and externally. Although the team is focused on a specific company process, strive to learn from competitors within and outside your industry.

For instance, for the past eight years, I have been improving customer experience operations in the financial industry. Therefore, I utilize products and services from other financial institutions, several fintech companies and mobile applications of numerous industries. I also pay close attention to FAANG (Facebook, Amazon, Apple, Netflix and Google) customer experience strategies, because these companies are elevating the user experience.

Paying attention to external businesses helps to quickly decipher internal strengths and weakenesss in order to proactively address them. In addition, I am an avid learner, and I read best practices of companies outside my industry that are considered to be world class. I also benchmark customer experiences from respected and admired brands like USAA,Starbucks, Disney, Southwest Airlines and Nike.

Take benchmarking a step further by participating in research studies with benchmarking organizations (JD Powers, Stevie Customer Service and Sales, or some of the top consulting companies).

Your Turn:

- How do you proactively sort through the data that is most important to the business?

- How could you potentially use a data collection plan to better understand business problems?

<u>Reflection:</u>

Think of a time when you did not use the all necessary data to solve a problem: what would you do differently?

ANALYZE

"In God we trust, all others must bring data."
W. Edwards Deming

In the analyze phase, we seek to understand the root cause of the problem. For instance, if we are digitizing customer experiences, we need to understand the problem that digitization solves. At this stage, several hypotheses have been developed; during the analysis phase, conduct analysis of the data to prove or discredit the hypotheses.

In simple terms, the goal of this phase is to perform analysis of the data gathered in order to understand the problem statement. It answers the "Why" questions that arise from the problem statement. Let's refer to the problem statement example #1 reviewed in an earlier chapter:

1. The software development team has been unable to meet delivery launch dates for the past 18 months. Major initiatives have been late by 3-6 months. The delay of product launches causes the project to go over budget by

20% (or over $1 million). Furthermore, there is high attrition rate of 18.2% on the development team and morale is low. Finally, product launch delays have an estimated revenue loss of potentially 20 million dollars annually.

Question: Why has the software team been unable to meet delivery launch dates?

Possible answers: The team is under-resourced by 10 people.

Possible answers: Testing has taken 30 days longer than expected.

Possible answers: We lack appropriate technical expertise.

Possible answers: The project scope was not well defined.

Possible answers: The vendor takes 15 days to resolve escalated issues.

Possible answers: Twenty-five percent more customer complaints were received during pilot testing, or there were insufficient users in the pilot tests.

During this phase, analytical tools commonly used are pareto charts, value added analysis, design of experiments (DOE), cause and effect diagrams, regression analysis, and hypothesis testing. Although various data points have been illustrated in chart form, ensure that all variables are accurately factored in, so that the root cause of the problems, and their viable solutions are better understood.

The analysis will help the team to develop conclusions to better prepare the brainstorming sessions and prioritization phase of the improvement phase.

- What is the hypothesis for the current problem within the organization?

- How do you validate a hypothesis?

- How do you arrive at the root cause? What can a team do in the analyze phase to understand root causes?

Reflection:

Was there ever a time that your organization developed a solution to a problem, but the solution did not completely resolve the issue? Why or why not?

IMPROVE

"Quality is never an accident; it is always the result of high intention, sincere effort, intelligent direction and skillful execution; it represents the wise choice of many alternatives." - William A. Foster

The improve phase of the process requires understanding the root cause acquired from the analyze phase. This phase helps determine the relationships of key variables to the project, which will aid in developing improvement ideas. All the demanding work done in the previous phases lacks merit without implementation.

This is the phase of the project where the team's work translates into action; the rubber meets the road. The solutions identified to reduce variation and to improve target performance are implemented and executed.

Engage in cross-functional collaborative efforts to acquire a multi-faceted understanding of the proposed solutions. There are various methods used to select and prioritize solutions. I recommend utilizing the solution matrix, which requires brainstorming the various solutions, and then rating each solution based on a weight scale.

Here is an example of a solution matrix:

CRITERIA AND WEIGHTS

	Easy to Implement	Quick	Customer Satisfaction	ROI	SUM
Solution	3	5	9	9	
A	15	15	36	36	102
B	3	15	9	18	45
C	6	15	18	18	57
D	6	5	27	18	56

Figure 6: Solution Matrix

In the table above, Solution A would be the best solution. In addition to conducting a solution matrix, a risk assessment should be evaluated. The weightings at the top illustrate the importance of that factor to the solution.

For Solution A

Easy to Implement: rated 5 (3 X 5=15)

Quick: rated 3 (5 x 3=15)

Customer Satisfaction: rated 4 (9 X 4 =36)

ROI: rated 4 (9 x 4=36)

The sum of 15+15+36+36=102.

Even after determining a solution, it is important to conduct a risk assessment of it. There is a risk assessment tool called FMEA, which stands for Failure, Mode, Effect, and Analysis.

The FMEA risk assessment:

- Identifies ways a product or process can fail
- Estimates the risk associated with specific causes
- Prioritizes the actions that should be taken to reduce risk
- Assesses the ability to detect the risk
- Evaluates the severity of the risk

A risk priority number (RPN) is the product of the severity, occurrence, and detection scores.

RPN = Severity X Occurrence X Detection:

Step 1: Identify the Potential Failure Modes and Causes

PROCESS STEP/INPUT	POTENTIAL FAILURE MODE
What is the process step or feature under investigation	In what ways could the step or feature go wrong?

Figure 7: First Step of FMEA Process

Step 2: Rate the Severity, Occurrence and Detection on a scale of 1-10 (See next three figures to acquire rating definitions)

Potential Failure	Scale	Potential Causes	Scale	Current Controls	Scale	RPN
What is the impact on the customer if this failure is not prevented or corrected?	Severity (1-10)	What causes the step or feature to go wrong? (how could it occur?)	Occurrence (1-10)	What controls exist that either prevent or detect the failure?	Detection (1-10)	Severity X Occurrence X Detection

Figure 8: Rating Severity, Occurrence, and Detection

SEVERITY

Effect	Criteria: Severity of Effect	Ranking
Hazardous - Without Warning	May expose client to loss, harm or major disruption - failure will occur **without** warning	10
Hazardous - With Warning	May expose client to loss, harm or major disruption - failure will occur **with** warning	9
Very High	Major disruption of service involving client interaction, resulting in either associate re-work or inconvenience to client	8
High	Minor disruption of service involving client interaction and resulting in either associate re-work or inconvenience to clients	7
Moderate	Major disruption of service not involving client interaction and resulting in either associate re-work or inconvenience to clients	6
Low	Minor disruption of service not involving client interaction and resulting in either associate re-work or inconvenience to clients	5
Very Low	Minor disruption of service involving client interaction that does not result in either associate re-work or inconvenience to clients	4
Minor	Minor disruption of service not involving client interaction and does not result in either associate re-work or inconvenience to clients	3
Very Minor	No disruption of service noticed by the client in any capacity and does not result in either associate re-work or inconvenience to clients	2
None	No Effect	1

Figure 9: Severity Definitions

OCCURRENCE

Probability of Failure	Time Period	Per Item Failure Rates	Ranking
Very High: Failure is almost inevitable	More than once per day	>= 1 in 2	10
	Once every 3-4 days	1 in 3	9
High: Generally associated with processes similar to previous processes that have often failed	Once every week	1 in 8	8
	Once every month	1 in 20	7
Moderate: Generally associated with processes similar to previous processes which have experienced occasional failures, but not in major proportions	Once every 3 months	1 in 80	6
	Once every 6 months	1 in 400	5
	Once a year	1 in 800	4
Low: Isolated failures associated with similar processes	Once every 1 - 3 years	1 in 1,500	3
Very Low: Only isolated failures associated with almost identical processes	Once every 3 - 6 years	1 in 3,000	2
Remote: Failure is unlikely. No failures associated with almost identical processes	Once Every 7+ Years	1 in 6000	1

Figure 10: Occurrence Definitions

DETECTION

Detection	Criteria: Likelihood the existence of a defect will be detected by process controls before next or subsequent process, -OR- before exposure to a client	Ranking
Almost Impossible	No known controls available to detect failure mode	10
Very Remote	Very remote likelihood current controls will detect failure mode	9
Remote	Remote likelihood current controls will detect failure mode	8
Very Low	Very low likelihood current controls will detect failure mode	7
Low	Low likelihood current controls will detect failure mode	6
Moderate	Moderate likelihood current controls will detect failure mode	5
Moderately High	Moderately high likelihood current controls will detect failure mode	4
High	High likelihood current controls will detect failure mode	3
Very High	Very high likelihood current controls will detect failure mode	2
Almost Certain	Current controls almost certain to detect the failure mode. Reliable detection controls are known with similar processes.	1

Figure 11: Detection Definitions

After the RPN is calculated and the high-risk areas identified, don't forget to develop methods to mitigate the risk, and implement a plan of action.

Action Recommended	Resp.	Actions Taken
What are the recommended actions for reducing the occurrence of the cause or improving detection?	Who is responsible for making sure the actions are completed?	What actions were completed (and when) with respect to the RPN?

Figure 12: Risk Mitigation Action Plan

As in the rest of the project, create a project plan for the risk mitigation opportunities that have been identified; include owners assigned to the actions and due dates. At this point, you are ready to conduct implementation. With well-defined business requirements and assigned resources, the initiative has a good chance of successful implementation.

- When you identify several viable solutions, how does the team determine the best one?

- Does your team conduct a risk assessment for each new process recommendation?

Reflection:

Have you ever experienced a solution implementation with hidden risks? How did the team recover? How would you prevent this in the future?

CONTROL

The control phase monitors the results and ensures that changes made are sustainable over time. To that end, it is necessary to standardize and document procedures, make sure all employees are trained, and communicate the project's results. In addition, the project team creates a plan for ongoing monitoring of the process and for reacting to any problems that may arise. Thus, in the control phase, solutions implemented in the improve phase are maintained long after the project has ended. The process map created during the measure phase should be reviewed and updated as necessary to reflect modifications which have occurred during the roll out. A deployment flowchart should also be developed to clarify roles and tasks. It is useful to produce a user guide which outlines the steps of the process. This is particularly important if multiple improvements were made and if the new process is substantially different from the original one.

The project team will ensure that everyone involved in the process receives proper training and communication. Training may involve classroom and/or online learning or may consist of distributing the process documentation. This is a fantastic opportunity to confirm that the process map and user guides are effective.

The results of the project can be monitored using a control chart that sets upper and lower control limits, an example is shown below:

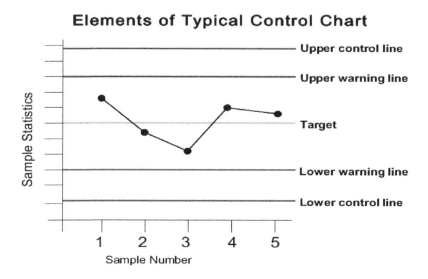

Figure 13: Control Chart

If a data point is above the upper control limit or below the lower control limit, the process is out of control; this could be due to a special cause and would require additional analysis to understand the cause of the deviation. However, when data points are within control limits, the process is in control and performing as expected, as in the sample control chart in figure 13. Even when a process is performing as expected, it is still important to avoid unknown deviations that may affect performance. There are also instances where it makes sense to adjust the control limits to reduce variation.

- How do you monitor results long after a project is completed?

- How could following the steps of the control phase add value to a new process initiative?

Reflection:

What goal did you forget while you were focused on other priorities?

SIX SIGMA SUMMARY TABLE

The previous sections provide a high-level overview of six-sigma. However, the table below provides a comprehensive overview of six-sigma tools.

DMAIC Phase Steps	Tools Used
D – Define Phase: Define the project goals and customer (internal and external) deliverables.	
• Define Customers (CTQs) • Develop Problem Statement, • Identify Champion, Process • Define Resources Obtain Organizational Develop Project Plan • Develop Process Map	Project Charter Process Flowchart SIPOC Diagram Stakeholder Analysis DMAIC Breakdown CTQ Definitions VOC
M – Measure Phase: Measure the process to determine current performance; quantify the problem.	
• Define Defect • Detailed Process Map • Develop Data Collection Validate the Measurement • Begin Developing Y=f(x) • Determine Process Capability	• Process Flowchart • Data Collection Plan/Example • Benchmarking • Measurement System Analysis/Gage R&R • Voice of the Customer • Process Sigma Calculation
A – Analyze Phase: Analyze and determine the root cause(s) of the defects.	
• Define Objectives • Identify Value/Non-Value Identify Sources of Variation • Determine Root Cause(s) • Determine Vital Few x's, Y=f(x) Relationship	• Histogram • Pareto Chart • Time Series/Run Chart • Scatter Plot • Regression Analysis • Cause and Effect/Fishbone • 5 Whys

	• Process Map Review
	• Statistical Analysis
	• Hypothesis Testing
	• Non-Normal Data Analysis

I – Improve Phase: Improve the process by eliminating defects.

Perform Design of Experiments	• Brainstorming
• Develop Potential Solutions	• Mistake Proofing
• Define Operating Tolerances Assess Failure Modes Validate Potential	• Design of Experiments
	• Pugh Matrix
	• QFD/House of Quality
• Improvement by Pilot Studies	• SimulFailure Modes and Effects Analysis (FMEA)
• Re-Evaluate Solutions	•

C – Control Phase: Control future process performance.

• Define and Validate Monitoring and Control System	• Process Sigma Calculation
• Develop Standards and Procedures	• Control Charts
• Implement Statistical Process Control	• Cost Savings Calculations
• Determine Process Capability	• Control Plan
• Develop Transfer Plan, Handoff to Process Owner	
• Verify Benefits, Cost Savings/Avoidance, Profit Growth	
• Close Project, Finalize Documentation	
• Communicate to Business, Celebrate	

Figure 14: Six- Sigma Summary Table

CUSTOMER EXPERIENCE

"Your most unhappy customers are your greatest source of learning." - Bill Gates

---

The customer can be called different things depending on the organization. In hospitals, the customer is the patient, at universities the customers are students, in credit unions the customer is the member. A customer is a person that receives or consumes products (goods or services) and chooses between various products and suppliers.

I recently went online to open a new bank account with one of the large financial institutions that boasts a digital first strategy. I assumed it would be a straightforward process that would take 10 minutes, instead there was a request for me to fax or mail my social security number, as well as send an identification card and signature. The process that I expected to take 10 minutes took over two weeks, so guess what I did? I opened the account with a company that provided a simpler process and enabled me to complete the end-to-end process on my mobile application within minutes.

One of the major transformation initiatives in various corporations is placing greater focus on the customer experience. Improving the customer experience enables acquisition of new customers and retention of current ones, which in turn increases revenue to the bottom line.

In the 2016 annual reports of Amazon, JP Morgan Chase, Apple, First Horizon National, Hilton and many others, customer experience continues to be a topic of emphasis. For that reason, some organizations have created a chief customer experience role whose sole focus is to develop a strategy for the end-to-end customer experience and to ensure that the enterprise strategy is aligned to achieve a superior customer experience.

To improve customer experience, leaders must be obsessed with eliminating customer problems and complaints. Thus, they identify root cause and address policy, product, and processes to resolve customer issues.

In addition, when there is a problem, organizations must have processes in place to quickly resolve the issue in a manner that exceeds the customer's expectations. That means associates delivering the customer experience must be empowered to make decisions in the moments that matter. A rule of thumb, is to design customer/user experiences that are simple, fast, and right.

Furthermore, customers desire connectivity on their terms; there is a definite line between the right amount and too much contact, which disengages the customer. For example, have you ever opted in for a company's automated email messages, but then unsubscribed because the information was too frequent and redundant? The trick is to provide the right amount of engagement.

As I examine ways to enhance the customer experience, the following objectives are top of mind:

- Maximize current resources

- Improve customer experience metrics

- Increase profitability

Customer experience transformation is more than providing a new channel with which to engage customers. For instance, most organizations today have an innovative voice response (IVR). Most IVRs can be powered by or enhanced with artificial intelligence. It is a good practice to evaluate its effectiveness on a regular basis and to make improvements.

Look for opportunities to simplify menu options, and understand the portions of your menu tree where the customer gives up and prefers to interact with a live agent. Most of all, track the percentage of IVR containment (the % of interactions that occur via an IVR), then determine how to increase it. A small percentage improvement lowers costs and frees up agents to handle the more complicated issues. In addition, evaluate the satisfaction and ease of use for each customer channel. Most of all, when the customer prefers to talk to a live person, the interaction should meet or exceed the customer expectations and preferably resolve the issue within the first contact.

Which Metric Matters?

I love numerical indicators, but metrics should not be evaluated in isolation; spend time assessing numerous variables. My husband and I love to travel, especially on Caribbean vacations. We select our destinations based on online research, recommendations from friends, and price. We recently saw a vacation package to a Caribbean destination that seemed like the bargain of the century. The ratings for the hotel were stellar (4.7 stars on a 5-point scale). However, as we started assessing further, we discovered that the package was available during the hurricane season; with that knowledge, the destination bargain was not a consideration.

During our research, we found another location with great reviews. I got excited. I told my husband "Wow, this all-inclusive package seems even better." The reviews were amazing (4.6 stars on a 5-point scale), it was not during hurricane season, and when we called the hotel, the receptionist was extremely pleasant (we would have given her a high customer satisfaction score, CSAT). However, a high CSAT does not necessarily mean a great vacation spot. My husband told me to look deeper beyond the 4.6 rating. Well, the comments seemed good but it was strange; it did not seem to be written by foreign travelers. Instead the reviews appeared to be written by owners of the resort. We then reviewed comments at TripAdvisor. The ratings at Trip Advisor are more closely aligned to net promoter scores (NPS). The truth was uncovered, most people on Trip Advisor would not recommend the resort, hence the rating of 2.3 stars.

The point of my story: net promoter scores tell more about the customer experience than CSAT scores. However, look at the details and variables to gain an accurate perspective.

For Customer experience leaders, pay close attention to

net promoter score (NPS), customer effort (CE), and customer loyalty index (CLI, or engagement). Although customer satisfaction is still utilized in a few organizations, CSAT serves as a "perceived satisfaction" and therefore does not provide the same level of customer commitment to a brand as NPS, CE or CLI. The following table provides an overview of the metrics:

Metric	Definition	Calculation	Overview
Net Promoter (NPS)	An index used to measure the willingness of customers to recommend a company's products or services to others	Measured on a 0-10 scale: "not at all likely" to "extremely likely" Percentage of promoters (9s or 10s) minus the percentage of detractors (0s to 6s) is the NPS.	Measures long term loyalty; based on several factors of the enterprise experience
Customer Effort (CES)	A straightforward way of measuring how customers feel about the effort it took for them to interact with your company's service	Typically asked on a 5-point scale from "much less effort than expected" to "much more effort than expected."	Covers one aspect of experience, and unrelated to emotional outcomes from human interaction

Customer Loyalty or Customer Engagement	Measure how engaged your customers are. The metric is represented by a number based on customer activity and usage of your product or service. The higher the number, the happier and more engaged the customer	Typically asked on a 5-point agree/disagree scale CLI covers satisfaction, retention and advocacy; CE aims for more emotional elements that indicate stickier relationships (such as effort and passion).	Varied questions, based on four measurements: 1. Retention 2. Effort 3. Advocacy 4. Passion
Customer Satisfaction	A traditional metric that measures the overall satisfaction of the interaction or service.	Question is measured on perceived quality: "overall, how satisfied are you with product or service"?	Measures short term loyalty; less precise and variable data, which often results in consistently high scores

Figure 15: Customer Experience Metrics and Definitions

Tracking metrics is the beginning of the process. Organizations should aim to understand the root cause of each metric and develop regular analysis and recommendations to improve it. NPS, CLI or CE should be evaluated at an enterprise level; the improvement opportunity is dependent on various cross-functional teams. For example, a customer may have a great interaction with an organization representative, but may not score a high NPS on a survey because the products and services are cumbersome, and require too much effort to reach a resolution when a problem occurs.

CSAT scores are higher, and easier to make

improvements, because CSAT typically depends on one interaction. However, NPS, CES and CLI have multiple interdependencies and are somewhat challenging to improve rapidly. To positively increase NPS, CES, or CLI metrics, product, process, policy, and technology changes need to be addressed. Thus, cross functional teams such as product, marketing, communications, legal, regulatory, technology, and operations teams collectively own the experience and collaboratively improve it.

Increasing Profitability

Focusing on customer experience (user experience, student experience, member experience, patient experience etc.), improves the bottom line revenue. Although linking the customer experience to profitability is not always obvious, companies that focus on customer experience acquire more customers, hence greater revenues. Customer asset management provides a bridge which can be used to estimate profitability.

Customer Asset Management

<u>New customers, volume and value</u>
Lost customers, volume and value

The customer asset management should be evaluated and shared with senior leaders, with a commitment to improve the experience that attains greater profitability. We analyze the data in order to know the "WHYS": Why does a customer do more business with a company? Why do they reduce the spend or relationship?

The best way to evaluate the metrics discussed is to understand the customer journey, and to establish a platform such as a customer contact council, that brings together cross-functional teams that collectively partner in order to improve the customer experience.

We can begin to tie digital transformation initiatives to the customer asset management, hence also improve customer experience. However, as we do so, we can add better focus to our digital road maps by maximizing current digital channels and improving customer experience, which better enables us to define the digital tools that improve profitability.

An example from a large financial institution:

I once led a customer experience team at a top 10 US financial institution; we were tasked with resolving the most complex customer issues. At the start of the initiative, less than 30% of customer escalations were resolved in a two-day period. We set a goal for 90% of all customer escalations to be resolved in 24 hours. The goal was bold and audacious, because the team came to the realization that if a customer had an issue with their finances, waiting five days was unacceptable.

The goal was based on the customer need. I felt that if a customer had an escalation with their bank and waited five days for a resolution, their expectations were unmet. By addressing performance issues, improving technology to track cases, coordinating with cross-functional teams, and designing new efficiencies, the team systematically achieved the goal.

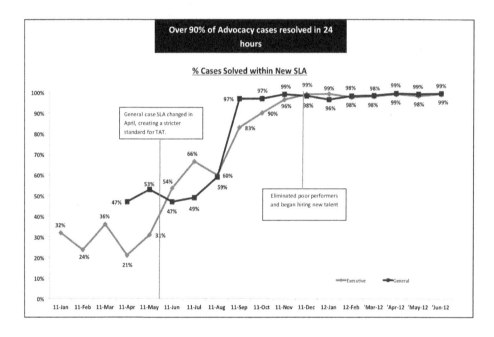

Figure 16: Service Level Improvements

The chart above illustrates the improvements a complaint team made by transforming the operations to improve complex resolutions. Although, the team realized a 40pt gain in net promoter score during the same time frame, there was no silver bullet. There was a focus on associates (recruit, train, retain, and develop) and attracting the right leaders for a customer-centric culture.

Most importantly, cross functional teams worked in small groups to improve processes such as fee refunds, fund availability, dormant accounts, and account closings. An improved retention team was created, and that team proactively retained customers' accounts of over $300 million annually.

Customer experiences (especially NPS) cannot be improved overnight, but with persistence and teamwork, customers can become the best promoters of a brand.

- Does your organization have a consistent understanding of customer experience? Why or why not?

- How can you influence a customer experience aligned to metrics and the culture?

Reflection:

What makes a customer experience memorable to you? What part of this experience stood out?

CUSTOMER ADVOCACY

"The key is to set realistic customer expectations, and then not to just meet them, but to exceed them — preferably in unexpected and helpful ways." – Richard Branson

---

Customer advocates study and understand the needs of a customer and help the company to satisfy those needs in a timely and cost-effective manner. The advocate serves as the voice of the customer and a trusted advisor. They know how to meet the customer's need in the moments that matter.

Characteristics of a great customer advocate:

- Thinks outside of the box
- Empowered to make decisions
- Understands the big picture
- Owns the customer experience
- Seasoned contact service professional

Thinks outside of the box: Customer advocates must

have multiple solutions to meet and anticipate the customer's needs. They think of creative solutions which might not be found in a training, policies or procedures manuals. They are great problem solvers who may deviate from a policy without putting the company at risk. This involves meeting the customer's need when it matters most.

Empowered: Customer advocates resolve the most complex issues at first contact. To do so, leaders provide the proper training, tools and escalation process for advocates.

Understands the big picture: Advocates understand the business strategy. For instance, not all customers are profitable. Even though advocates primarily win customers, they know when to fire a customer or when a customer's request does not fit the corporation's business model.

Owns the customer experience: Advocates are willing take ownership of the customer interaction; their conversation is proactive, not reactive, and reduces customer effort.

Seasoned: Customer professionals do not become advocates overnight. They have enough experience to remain calm during the most complicated and uncomfortable customer scenarios. Furthermore, advocates develop a deep knowledge of customer preferences and company offerings.

If an organization lacks the competencies of a customer advocate, there is still hope. Leaders can develop associates into advocates by modeling a customer centric culture. By focusing on the end-to-end customer journey, identifying the breakdowns, and implementing sustainable solutions, the role of the advocate becomes simplified. The more product designers create experiences that are simple, right, and fast, the easier it will be to consistently exceed customer expectations.

In summary, the customer advocate model can be represented by the chart below:

Course of Action	Activities	Company Logic	Customer Perception
React	Increase retention	We need to stop the bleeding	"I called to cancel they made an offer, I could not refuse"
Detect	Take action to prevent churn	Identify who is likely to leave and prevent it	"I was about to cancel when they presented me with an interesting offer"
Prevent	Identify root cause and eliminate the problem	Ensure customer do not have negative experiences	"I have no reason to switch"
Differentiate	Make a unique promise to customers	Distinguish our services so customers become loyal	They tell friends and family " You should switch to this product/service"

Figure 17: Stages of Customer Advocacy

In many organizations, leaders are focused on improving

the customer experience, so defining the role of the advocate is important. Each stage is important in the evolution cycle. In the instances of react and detect, if a clear strategy is not executed customers will leave. When we prevent a bad customer experience, we are proactively understanding the problems that exist and eliminating the issues. The ideal position is to differentiate the experience by providing a compelling promise that connects with the hearts and minds of customers, which in turn influences customers to make a purchase.

Southwest Airlines has found wonderful ways to differentiate its customer experience, as a result their passengers become the airlines' biggest advocates. My mother recently purchased a plane ticket from Southwest Airlines. After the purchase, she needed to change her travel dates. She was concerned because most airlines charge change fees of approximately $200 or more. However, Southwest Airlines' policy allowed her to change her flight at no cost, and there was no charge for two checked luggage bags. She was elated, and called several family members (including me) to rant about Southwest Airlines' customer-friendly differentiated policies (i.e., change fees and baggage fees).

The ideal state to transform the customer experience is to deliver a differentiated experience—one that makes a unique promise to customers. Southwest Airlines make a unique promise to its customers, for that reason it gains higher profitability that many of its competitors. When a differentiated customer experience is delivered, customers become loyal and tell their friends about the product/service. It is at the stage of delivering a differentiated experience that a net promoter is achieved.

Passion for Excellence: Service from the Heart

On an extraordinarily frigid February morning in Texas (Yes, Texas has a few of those days), I began a new role as an advocacy leader. It was my first day at a new company and I was tasked with the terrific opportunity of transforming the customer experience of a retail bank. My boss empowered me to take whatever action needed to improve customer satisfaction and manage compliance. I walked around the contact center operation to learn about my new team. Once again, team morale seemed to be waning (sounds familiar, doesn't it?). Despite their politeness and deep knowledgebase, the team was not engaged, and lacked passion. It was a formula for lackluster results and high employee churn.

I walked back to my office to try and figure out what

was going on; the phone rang. It was one of the leaders of the east coast team. Her tone was nervous. Apparently, her team had recently been acquired by the company through a buyout, and roles had already been eliminated to reduce redundancy and expense. Anxiety levels were at a fever pitch; I immediately recognized that transforming the customer experience would be challenging.

How was I going to transform this team and improve the customer experience when it was apparent they lacked passion for their work? I sat in the office for hours agonizing over irrelevant metrics, dispassionate people, and misapplied technology. I started walking around the contact center floor and overheard one of the associates speaking to a customer. She sounded excited and upbeat. After the call, I complimented her on having a great call and asked her what was the secret to her success? She said, I have a heart for people and I'm passionate about helping them. I quickly gathered my leadership team together and we began working to establish a new positioning theme for our business unit. We wanted to embody the spirit of excellence and create an environment where everyone desired to be the best. Our rallying cry was:

> *"Passion for Excellence, Service from the Heart"*

Our slogan inspired the team members and rallied a transformation that increased customer satisfaction, net promoter scores, and led to four Customer Service and Sales Stevie Awards. We created a logo to consistently remind us why we were there. A transformational change occurred beyond the advocacy organization, it crept into other business units as well. It motivated the team to work at their full potential and constantly challenged my leadership team, business partners, colleagues and executives to provide the necessary tools and emotional environment that we needed to deliver an experience that demonstrated a passion for excellence and service from the heart.

Figure 18: The Team Logo

We used this statement to define our attitude. We then integrated this into all our training, quality management, and team discussions. The logo was used on certificates, trophy awards, banners, and email signatures. The motto was used during new hire training and included in job descriptions. Banners and balloons were placed all over the organization with the words "Passion for Excellence... Service from the Heart."

This motto inspired individuals throughout the organization. It was easy to remember and motivated the team to exemplify behaviors that illustrate a "Passion for Excellence...Service from the Heart" culture. A central idea inspired a transformational effort with a positive internal impact that became noticeable to our external customers. Our organization began to attract top talent, attrition dropped, associate engagement increased, customer experience metrics increased, and our cost per contact dropped significantly. We worked hard and had fun in the process of transforming the customer advocacy department. The department town halls were creative; the events recognized top performance, celebrated successes, communicated changes, and enabled team members to share ideas.

When I received the 2013 Stevie Customer Service & Sales, Contact Center of the Year leader award, I was most grateful that the team was willing to follow my leadership and I was also grateful to those who worked with me to achieve aggressive goals.

2013 Customer Service and Sales Award Ceremony

Leaders celebrating with their teams at year end

Coffee mugs reminding associates of the team motto

Making town halls creative and engaging to convey a business plan

So how did we transform the organization to one of high performance and net promoter improvement? A strategy map with emphasis on people, process, technology and benchmarks. However, I focused first on the PEOPLE.

- Associates: There needs to be an associate profile that drives great customer experience; these attributes must be known throughout the organization.
- Training: A component of the training must focus on soft skills that promote the culture as well as a digital

experience. Training should include videos, chat, mobile applications etc.

- Recruiting: Hire associates that fit the culture and are adaptable to change. Develop a recruitment strategy that might be strikingly different from the current ideal candidate profile. Thus, the channels to recruit talent may also differ.

- Recognition: Associates should be motivated in their work and rewarded for promoting the right behaviors that lead to desired outcomes. Although monetary rewards are needed, intrinsic rewards provide lasting impact as well.

There are many ways give associates recognition, here are some examples:

- Handwritten "thank you" notes from the executives or the direct leader
- Associate names listed in company newsletters or on the intranet
- Public praise at team meetings or town halls
- Donuts or cupcakes for the entire site with the highest business results
- Team lunch top performers sent to a conference, seminar or workshop of their choice

- Associate can represent the department at an interdepartmental meeting
- Associates work on special projects or community service programs
- "Hall of Fame" for top performing teams
- Gift certificates
- A "performance points" system that enables associates to redeem points for cash
- Pick a work schedule for top annual performer
- Plaques or framed certificates of achievement
- Tickets to movies, concerts, sporting events, etc.
- All-expense-paid weekend away at a local resort
- A day at a spa
- "Agent Appreciation Week" celebrations
- An annual awards dinner
- Increased opportunities for empowerment and self-management
- Names/photos of high performing associates posted at a visible location

Career development

Transformation is a continuous process, as the team achieves greater business accomplishments, team mates reach a new level of potential, and seek growth opportunities. Thus, it is important to develop clear plans to support career progression. We provided resources and promotion opportunities internally and externally. Although it was sometimes sad to see top performers move on to other roles, it was fulfilling to realize that we developed individuals that were sought after throughout the company and continued to conduct their work with a "Passion for Excellence and Service from the Heart".

- Does your team have a rallying cry or mission statement? Why or why not?

- How could a rallying cry inspire a team?

Reflections:

Have you ever worked for a mission oriented organization? What did it feel like?

CUSTOMER JOURNEYS

A customer journey map is an illustration of the end-to-end steps customers go through to engage with a company. The customer journey highlights the specific steps that customers take when using a product, service, or any combination. Customer journeys provide insights into the small and grandiose things that work with customers, as well as the cumbersome ones.

In addition, the journey shows the full life cycle to highlight a clear understanding of how it feels to walk in the customer's shoes. Journey mapping helps to pinpoint and document key moments of the customer's experience.

Documentation of each stage of the journey magnifies interactions along the way and exposes the emotional highs and lows of the customer's experience. It is important to properly document each stage. The purpose of the customer journey is to:

- Understand the customers' experience from their perspective
- Evolve focus from touch points to journeys
- Help determine where to listen to the voice of the customer (VOC) along the journey
- Build customer empathy
- Create or redesign interactions
- Magnify the customers' complaints and dissatisfactions

The customer journey provides a simplified method to improve the customer experience by combining the journey with data analytics; it tells a story. As you outline the steps, highlight the ones that balance customer experience and profitability.

- What can you begin to do to capture the customer's journey?

Reflection:

Have you ever been surprised at poor experiences your company delivers to customers? What was done about it?

FROM THE INSIDE OUT

"The most important journey you will take in your life will usually be the one of self-transformation. Often, this is the scariest because it requires the greatest changes in your life."
—*Shannon L. Alder*

Are you ready to transform an organization and lead a team to new heights? Before sharing an incredible transformation strategy, self-evaluation is essential to see if your temperament and leadership style supports a transformational culture.

Expand your self-awareness abilities and transform YOU.

I noted earlier that many executives assume they are the solution, yet in many instances, they are contributors to the problem. We cannot assume that everything else needs change without first examining ourselves. What if your communication style is a barrier? Do your peers and team members trust you? Do you understand what motivates people? Have you considered what motivates you?

One method I use to help my self-transformation effort is by developing a personal mission statement. In my efforts to increase my self-awareness, my value statement keeps me aligned to my personal objectives and goals. It is a statement that simply says, "I desire to walk alongside others and enable them to reach a destination that far exceeds expectations." This statement is the guiding principle that enables me to transform operations, deliver results that exceed expectations, improve enterprise customer experiences, and even inspire teams, friends and family members to reach their full potential. I routinely revisit my value statement to evaluate my ability to fulfill it. It is also a good practice to seek constructive feedback from trusted peers and from professional coaches.

In addition to creating and realigning my value statement, I am deliberate about taking "me" time. I have established times to exercise, meditate, pray, reflect, laugh, dream and take time off work. This time allows me to remove myself from the normal hectic day-to-day situations and rejuvenate. By establishing "me time", I acquire the balance I need to think clearly.

Finally, I surround myself with people that bring out the best in me. I am fortunate to have a husband that propels me to keep up with innovative technologies, take risks, and remain calm when things don't go as planned. We all need people in our circle at work and home that help to challenge us and keep us grounded.

Transformation is not easy, because there is no simple recipe for change. Anyone who touts a quick and painless transformation process has never led transformation. Transformational leaders are quite often misunderstood; they can/will face tremendous adversity. Thus, transformational leaders need to be deliberate in staying on course and remaining true to their values.

Change can evoke fear and negative responses. These fears can manifest into corporate political firestorms and misunderstandings that not only threaten the success of an initiative, they could even decrease a leader's tenure in an organization. You must look deep inside yourself to conjure up the mental fortitude required to successfully implement transformation initiatives.

Remember, leaders change more than processes, they change cultures. The impact of these changes can move far beyond the profit and loss statements of a corporation. It can impact employees, communities, customers, and competitors. Regardless of the organization's size or the industry, implementing change is challenging. Transformation leaders find ways to stay motivated and positive. Some leaders listen to self-help tapes, read business articles, and attend conferences or networking events to keep positive and stay current on industry trends.

I personally prescribe to the power of positive speaking. Instead of speaking negatively, I use positive sentences to help set an optimistic tone to encourage others. I use the next few phrases to motivate myself as well as others:

Be the captain, when everyone else is
content with being in the crew.

Be the leader when everyone else is too scared to lead and
would rather be followers.

Trust yourself when everyone doubts you.

Winners never quit and quitters never win

Be a lion when all others are being the sheep.

Be extraordinary, don't take anything or anyone for granted.

Remain motivated even when you fail. Instead of being discouraged, take the failure as a learning opportunity. Discover why the effort failed and try again. Remember, the organization would not have hired you if you didn't have the ability. Find a systemic approach to success and make it your own. Johannes Gutenberg, Thomas Edison, Elizabeth Cady Stanton, George Washington Carver, and Jack Kilby were all transformationalists that perfected a systemic approach to change. They were met with challenges, but they continued their march for change. Of course, I am not comparing what many of us do to the creation of the printing press or the integrated computer chip. I am saying that their push for change started with a desire to help others.

Transformation of any kind is challenging. Advocating change should start from within. Once the changes have been implemented and perfected, the results will be proven by your data and empirical evidence. What happens once the results are in? The cycle continues. It's a continuous process of change, so the adage penned by the ancient Greek Philosopher Heraclitus, "Nothing is constant except change" is accurate. I would add one thing to Heraclitus' quote. Change begins from the inside out.

Transformation happens from the inside out.

GLOSSARY

A

Analyze The third phase of a six-sigma process that conducts extensive analysis and creates charts and graphs to deepen the understanding of the project.

Application Program Interface (API) A set of routines, protocols, and tools for building software applications. An API specifies how software components should interact. Additionally, APIs are used when programming graphical user interface (GUI) components.

B

Bot Also known as an Internet Bot, web robot, or WWW robot, it is a software application that runs automated tasks (scripts) over the Internet. Typically, bots perform tasks that are both simple and structurally repetitive at a much higher rate than would be possible for a human alone.

Charter Each project begins with an idea, a vision, or a business opportunity—and that is the starting point that must be associated with your organization's business objectives.

CLI (Customer Loyalty Index) This is a standardized

metric to track customer loyalty over time, and it incorporates the values of NPS, repurchasing, and upselling.

Control The last phase of the six-sigma phase designed to monitor the results and ensure that they are sustainable over time.

CTQs (critical to quality) These are the key measurable characteristics of a product or process whose performance standards or specification limits must be met to satisfy the customer. They align improvement or design efforts with customer requirements.

Customer Advocate A person or function entrusted by the management of a firm to study the needs of its customers and help the firm to satisfy them in a timely and cost-effective manner. Also, a person employed by a company to speak out on behalf of your customer's interests; the advocate is a trusted advisor that resolves complicated customer complaints in a manner that exceeds the customers expectations.

Customer Asset Management Measures the number of customers gained versus customers lost.

Customer Effort Score (CES) A metric to measure customer service satisfaction with one single question. The underlying thought is that service organizations create loyal customers by reducing customer effort.

Customer Experience Officer (CXO) The link between the customer and the organization. "A chief experience officer (CXO) is the officer responsible for the overall user experience (UX) of an organization."

Customer Journey (CJ) An illustration of the end-to-end steps that customers go through in engaging with a company. The customer journey can be the steps with a product, an online experience, retail experience, or a service, or any combination of these.

D

Define First phase of a six-sigma process that outlines the problem statement of an initiative, as well as its scope and goals.

Digital Describes electronic technology that generates, stores, and processes data in terms of two states: positive and non-positive.

Digital transformation The profound and accelerating transformation of business activities, processes, competencies, and models, to fully leverage the changes and opportunities of digital technologies, and their impact across society in a strategic and prioritized way, with present and future shifts in mind.

DMADV A six-sigma methodology to design new processes. Stands for Define, Measure, Analyze, Improve and Verify.

DMAIC A six-sigma methodology to improve current processes. Stands for Define, Measure, Analyze, Improve and Control.

F

FANNG An acronym for the five most popular and best high performing tech stocks in the market, namely Facebook, Apple, Amazon, Netflix, and Alphabet's Google.

Fintech Computer programs and other technology used to support or enable banking and financial services.

FMEA (failure, mode, effects and analysis) A risk assessment tool utilized to determine possible failures in a design or process and factor methods to detect and identify the severity of the failures.

I

Improve Fourth phase of a six-sigma process that uses various tools to brainstorm viable solutions, prioritize the solutions to the initiative, and identify the risks.

Internet of Things (IoT)   The interconnection via the Internet of computing devices embedded in everyday objects, enabling them to send and receive data.

IVR (Innovative Voice Response) An automated telephony system that interacts with callers, gathers information, and routes calls to the appropriate recipient.

M

Measure Second phase of a six-sigma process that outlines the data that will be relevant to the project.

N

Net promoter score (NPS) A management tool that can be used to gauge the loyalty of a firm's customer relationships. It serves as an alternative to traditional customer satisfaction research and claims to be correlated with revenue growth.

Q

Quick wins now Phraseology developed by Alice Sesay Pope that encourages process experts to implement no brainer solutions quickly, and eliminate analysis paralysis.

S

Six-sigma is a set of management techniques intended to improve business processes by greatly reducing the probability that an error or defect will occur.

Statistical Six sigma Measures the capability of a process to deliver a defect-free product or service. Six Sigma means a failure rate of 3.4 parts per million or 99.9997%.

Solution Matrix A framework that can be used to evaluate solution ideas against specific criteria.

T

Transformation A complete change that reconfigures or redesigns something so that it becomes different from its starting point.

U

User experience (UX) Encompasses all aspects of the end-*user's* interaction with the company, its services, and its products. The first requirement for an exemplary *user experience* is to meet the exact needs of the customer.

V

VOC (voice of the customer) A term used to describe the in-depth process of capturing a customer's expectations, preferences, and aversions.

Made in the USA
Las Vegas, NV
25 August 2022

54018070R00075